YOUR LAND
AND
MY LAND

We Visit

BRAZIL

Kathleen

Tracy

Mitchell Lane

PUBLISHERS

P.O. Box 196
Hockessin, Delaware 19707

YOUR LAND AND MY LAND

Brazil
Chile
Colombia
Cuba
Dominican Republic
Mexico
Panama
Peru
Puerto Rico
Venezuela

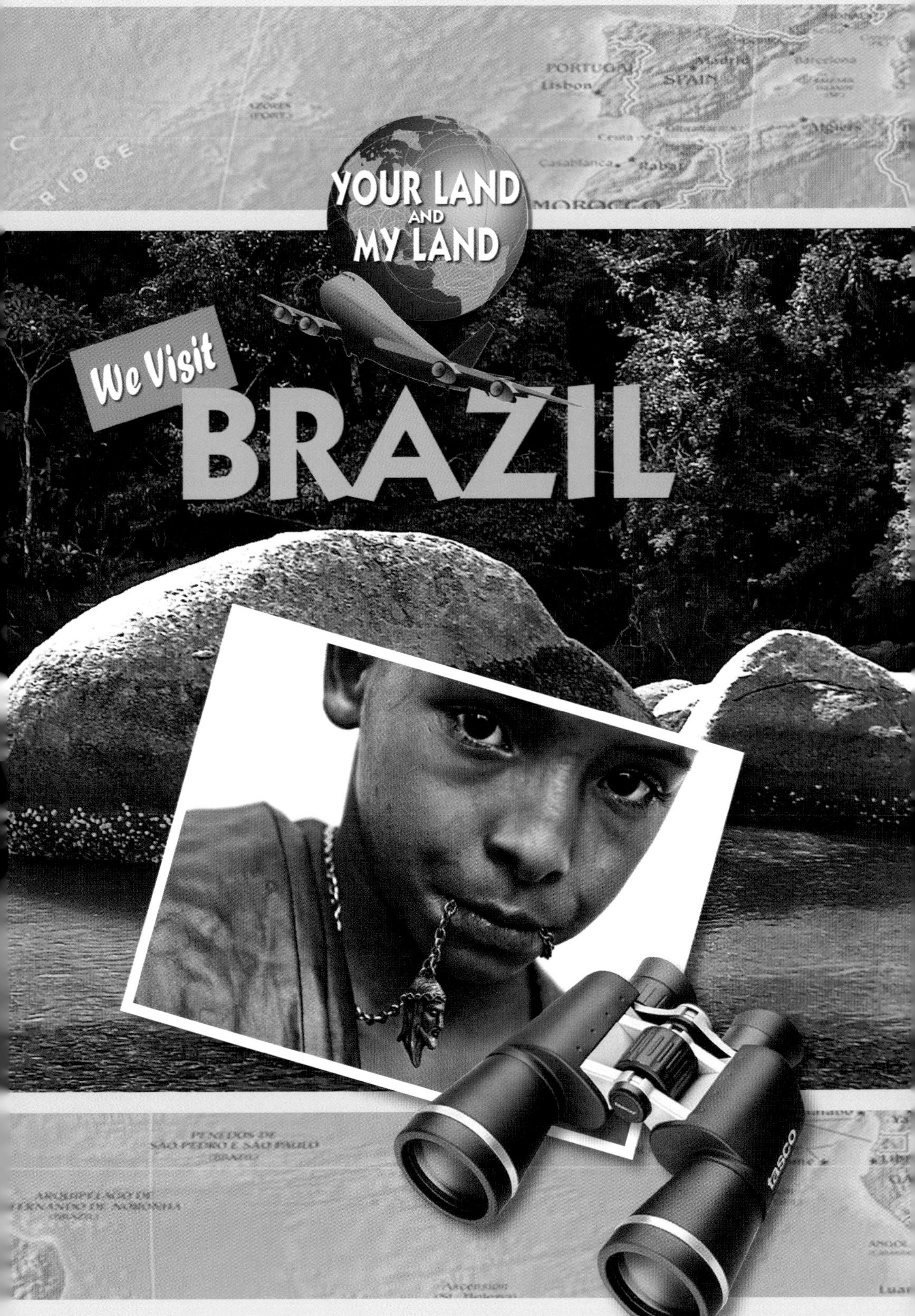
YOUR LAND AND MY LAND
We Visit
BRAZIL
PORTUGAL
Lisbon
Madrid
SPAIN
Barcelona
Casablanca
Rabat
MOROCCO
RIDGE
PENEDOS DE
SÃO PEDRO E SÃO PAULO
(BRAZIL)
ARQUIPÉLAGO DE
FERNANDO DE NORONHA
(BRAZIL)
Ascension
tasco

Mitchell Lane

PUBLISHERS

Printing   1   2   3   4   5   6   7   8   9

Library of Congress Cataloging-in-Publication Data
Tracy, Kathleen.
  We visit Brazil/by Kathleen Tracy.
      p. cm. — (Your land and my land)
  Includes bibliographical references and index.
  ISBN 978-1-58415-887-5 (library bound)
  1. Brazil—Juvenile literature. I. Title.
  F2508.5.T73 2010
  981—dc22

                                                                2010026961

PUBLISHER'S NOTE: This story is based on the author's extensive research, which she believes to be accurate. Documentation of this research is on page 61.

The Internet sites referenced herein were active as of the publication date. Due to the fleeting nature of some web sites, we cannot guarantee they will all be active when you are reading this book.

                                                                PLB

Contents

Introduction

The term *Latin America* has no single definition. In some cases, it refers to the countries south of the United States. Other times, it refers to Central and South America and all the Caribbean countries. But most commonly, and for our purposes, it describes the western hemisphere countries where Spanish and Portuguese—and to a lesser extent French—are the primary spoken languages. These countries in the Americas were once part of either the Spanish or the Portuguese empire.

Latin America encompasses a wide geographic area, from the Strait of Magellan at the tip of Argentina to the eastern Caribbean. Although Latin American countries share common languages, a common religion (Catholicism), and similar colonial backgrounds, each country has a unique history and distinctive culture that is the foundation of its national identity. In this book we'll explore Brazil, a land that blends past and present into a country poised for the future.

Rio de Janeiro

The Regions and Countries of Latin America

Caribbean: Cuba, the Dominican Republic, and Puerto Rico
North America: Mexico
Central America: Belize, Costa Rica, El Salvador, Guatemala, Honduras, Nicaragua, Panama
South America: Argentina, Bolivia, Brazil, Chile, Colombia, Ecuador, French Guiana, Guyana, Paraguay, Peru, Suriname, Uruguay, Venezuela

LATIN AMERICA

FYI FACT:

The Amazon River is named after the Amazons, female warriors in Greek mythology. Historians believe European explorers came up with the name after they were attacked by native tribal war parties that included many women.

About one-fourth of the world's known plant species are found in Brazil. The southern states are known for their exotic flowers and vast pine forests.

Country Overview

Welcome to Brazil!

In 1500 when the first Portuguese explorers landed on what is now known as Brazil, they mistakenly thought it was an island and named it Ilha de Vera Cruz, or "Island of the True Cross." When they realized they had actually found a new continent, they renamed it Terra de Santa Cruz, "Land of the Holy Cross."

Slightly larger than Australia, Brazil is the largest country by area and population in South America and the fifth largest in the world. It spans much of the eastern South American coast. It has the most advanced economy in the region, although there is a vast gap between the haves and have-nots.

Ten percent of the country is in the northern hemisphere, the rest is in the southern hemisphere. It is so large that it is adjacent to every country on mainland South America except Ecuador and Chile. Brazil is made up of 26 states and a federal district, similar to Washington, D.C.

You might be surprised to learn the country was named after a tree. Once explorers became more familiar with the terrain, they noticed the region was thickly covered with a particular type of tree. The tree's wood was a distinctive deep red color and became known as *pau brasil,* which loosely translated means "wood the color of glowing coal." It is now known as brazilwood.

It didn't take the Europeans long to discover that if the wood was ground into powder, it could be used to make paints and fabric dyes

Brazilwood
(*Caesalpinia echinata*)

of the same distinctive color as red-hot embers. Brazilwood became the region's first important export. Over the next four centuries, millions of the trees were cut down and processed into dyes and paints. In Italy, the color of the brazilwood paints was called *verzino* and was made in different shades. Many of the world's most famous artists used paints made from brazilwood.

Brazil was a Portuguese colony for more than 300 years. It gained independence in the early nineteenth century and established a monarchy. From the late 1800s to the middle of the next century, Brazil struggled through political and social upheaval but eventually adopted a democratic government.

Brazil is a country of contradictions. While it possesses one of South America's strongest economies, it has the largest wealth disparity,

Almost 200 million people live in Brazil, making it the fifth most populous country in the world. School is mandatory, but in rural areas the school calendar is scheduled so that it won't interfere with planting and harvesting season.

with 5 percent of the population possessing 85 percent of the wealth. The country has the world's largest reserves of tropical forest, fresh-water, and biodiversity, and it is one of the largest contributors of greenhouse gases. It is one of the most populous countries, but the urban areas are clustered on the coast, so the majority of the country is sparsely populated with limited technological infrastructure. It has the highest voting rate in the Americas but only because voting is mandatory by law. The country's diverse population is the source of both Brazil's vibrant culture and its social struggles. It is a Republic still in search of a consistent political identity.

Brazil is a modern country that embraces its colonial past as much as the future in its quest to remain Latin America's premier country for years to come.

FYI FACT:

The Amazon rain forest is home to 30 percent of all plant and animal life on earth.

WHERE IN THE WORLD IS BRAZIL?

Brazil is part of Latin America, which spans a wide geographic area, from the Strait of Magellan at the tip of Argentina to the eastern Caribbean. Ten percent of the country is in the northern hemisphere, the rest is in the southern hemisphere.

BRAZIL FACTS AT A GLANCE

Rufous-bellied Thrush

Full country name: Federative Republic of Brazil

Languages: Portuguese (official), Spanish, English, French

Population: 186 million (2009 estimate); the 2000 census reported 170 million

Area: 3,286,473 square miles (8,511,965 square kilometers), slightly larger than Australia

Capital City: Brasilia (2,529,580 pop.)

Government: Federative Republic

Ethnic makeup: White (53.7%); mulatto (38.5%); black (6.2%)

Religions: Roman Catholicism; Protestantism; Spiritualism; Bantu/voodoo

Climate: Mostly tropical, but more temperate in southern area of the country

Average rainfall: Varies between regions (see Chapter 3)

Lowest point: Sea level (Atlantic Ocean)

Highest point: Pico da Neblina (9,888 feet/3,014 meters)

Longest River: Amazon River

National flower: Flowering araguaney (*ipê-amarelo*)

National bird: Rufous-bellied Thrush (*Sabiá-laranjeira*)

National tree: Brazilwood (*Pau brasil*)

Brazil's States: Acre, Alagoas, Amapa, Amazonas, Bahia, Ceara, Distrito Federal, Espirito Santo, Goias, Maranhao, Mato Grosso, Mato Grosso do Sul, Minas Gerais, Para, Paraiba, Paraná, Pernambuco, Piaui, Rio de Janeiro, Rio Grande do Norte, Rio Grande do Sul, Rondonia, Roraima, Santa Catarina, São Paulo, Sergipe, Tocantins

Flag: The Brazilian flag was designed by artist Decio Vilares and was officially adopted on November 19, 1889. The inscription across the blue sky, *Ordem e Progresso,* means "Order and Progress." The phrase is attributed to French philosopher Augusto Comte. The green background represents the natural resources such as the Amazon rain forest. The yellow diamond specifically symbolizes the country's gold reserves and generally Brazil's overall wealth. Each star on the blue sky represents one of the 26 Brazilian states plus the federal district of the country's capital. They are positioned to re-create the alignment of stars present in the night sky over Rio de Janeiro on the night of November 15, 1889.

Source: *CIA World Factbook,* "Brazil"

Before the Europeans arrived, there were an estimated 2,000 nations and tribes in Brazil. Most vanished as a result of colonization, and it is estimated that only 200 tribes remain.

There are two schools of thought about who originally settled the region we now know as Brazil. The longest held scenario is that Brazil's indigenous population was descended from the first wave of North Asians who crossed into North America across the Bering Strait at the end of the Ice Age. This would have been between 13,000 and 17,000 years ago. These tribes eventually migrated down to South America.

However, archaeological findings seem to challenge that long-held view. Remains of ancient settlements have been unearthed that could be up to 40,000 or 50,000 years old—too old to be from the Bering Strait tribes. Plus, the bones are more similar to African or Aboriginal in morphology. The new theory is that these older Amerinds were in Brazil first, having arrived from the south, and were later overrun by or absorbed into the Amerinds of North Asia origin.

Part of the uncertainty is that Brazil's indigenous tribes did not keep written records. Another obstacle for archaeologists is that the area's high humidity and the type of soil are not good for preserving relics such as structures or even human bones. The history of the area prior to 1500 has been assembled in part by a lot of educated inferences and assorted archaeological evidence.

The European explorers, on the other hand, kept many records. Pedro Cabral was accompanied by an official diarist named Pêro Vaz de Caminha. From him we know that when Cabral landed in what is

The best-known fish of the Amazon is the piranha. Despite stories about man-eating piranhas, attacks on humans are rare. Most species are herbivores, eating fruit and seeds.

now the state of Bahia, thousands of indigenous tribes lived along the coastal areas and along rivers.

It is estimated that at the beginning of the sixteenth century, there were upwards of 2,000 tribes in Brazil. The majority were hunter-gatherers who also planted some crops. Archaeologists describe the tribes as seminomadic, and they relied heavily on the resources of the forest. The woods were filled with game animals; the rivers were thick with fish. For thousands of years the forest sustained the indigenous people.

The arrival of the Europeans was the beginning of the indigenous tribes' demise. Intermarriage and diseases introduced by the explorers and settlers, such as measles, the flu, and tuberculosis, decimated the

Amerind population. Also, within a few hundred years of European settlements, much of their natural food resources were depleted, forcing hunters to venture farther and farther into the forest.

In addition to a growing number of Portuguese settlers, a wave of colonists from the Netherlands arrived in the early 1600s, drawn by the seemingly unlimited natural resources. The Dutch were not made welcome by the Portuguese colonists, and they eventually relocated elsewhere.

The settlements were largely restricted to the coast. Most rivers run north and south, so ships by and large cannot travel very far inland. The exception is the Amazon, which allows access about 1,000 miles (1,600 kilometers) inland to Manaus.

The main crops of these early colonists were sugarcane and brazilwood. Brazil was also rich in minerals and precious metals, so gold mining was also a growing industry. With the native population dramatically declining, people from Africa were imported as slaves to fill the labor needs.

In November 1807, Napoleon Bonaparte's army invaded Portugal, prompting the Portuguese royal family, including Queen Maria and her son, Dom Pedro I, to flee and relocate in Brazil. They made the newly dubbed Kingdom of Brazil the center of Portuguese government.

In 1821, João—and the Portuguese government—returned to Lisbon and left his son Dom Pedro in charge of Brazil. With João back in Lisbon, the government intended to return Brazil's status to a colony. To João's surprise, his son declared Brazil's independence on September 7, 1822. This resulted in a very minor conflict known as the Brazilian War of Independence.

On August 29, 1825, the Brazilian Empire's independence was officially recognized by Britain and Portugal. The empire was led by Dom Pedro I. Rather than achieving

FYI FACT:

After the end of the U.S. Civil War, many former Confederates moved to Brazil so that they could live in a place that still allowed slavery.

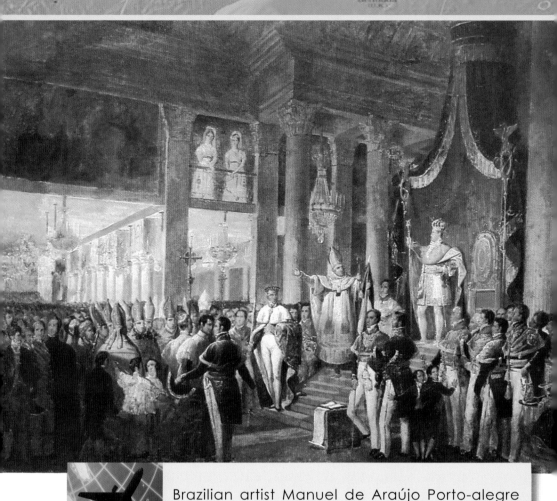

Brazilian artist Manuel de Araújo Porto-alegre painted *The Consecration of Dom Pedro II* after he was commissioned to do so in 1840. About 160 people attended the ceremony.

true independence, Brazil just maintained its status as the other half of the Portuguese Empire. Pedro I was succeeded by his son, Pedro II, who abolished slavery in 1888.

In the late nineteenth and early twentieth century, over 5 million European, Arab, and Japanese people immigrated to Brazil. The influx of immigrants was instrumental in the country's industrialization and social development.

Pedro II

Pedro de Alcântara João Carlos Leopoldo Salvador Bebiano Francisco Xavier de Paula Leocádio Miguel Gabriel Rafael Gonzaga—better known as Pedro II—was the second, and last, Brazilian emperor. He reigned for nearly fifty years and is now considered by many to be the greatest Brazilian leader in the country's history.

Pedro was born December 2, 1825, in Rio de Janeiro. His father, Pedro I, abdicated when Pedro was only five years old. Brazil was ruled by regency, a group of people who ruled until the young boy was old enough to assume the throne.

Pedro II at age 54, 1880

Pedro became the official ruler in 1840, when he was fourteen years old. Among his goals was to educate Brazilians, and he supported national public education. He led by example: He was a voracious reader, studied astronomy, and learned many foreign languages, such as Sanskrit and Hebrew. He also mastered the Brazilian Indian dialect, Tupi-Guarani. The young emperor managed to maintain peace and economic stability, earning respect as a leader. His reign was ultimately undermined by the abolition of slavery in 1888 and an increasing public—and military—sentiment against the power of the monarchy.

In November 1889, Pedro's throne was overthrown in a bloodless coup led by General Manuel Deodoro da Fonseca. Pedro was forced into exile and settled in Paris, feeling betrayed. He died two years later.

The French government honored him with a state funeral that was attended by very few Brazilians. It would be thirty years before Pedro's remains were returned to Brazil and buried in the Cathedral at Petrópolis, located in the mountains above Rio de Janeiro.

Originally Parque Lage was the home of industrialist Henrique Lage, whose wife was singer Gabriella Besanzoni. In the 1960s the property became a public park. The mansion houses the Visual Arts School of Parque Lage and a café.

Politics and Government

Brazil is a republic with a multiparty political system. Democratic elections are held for the president, federal legislatures, state governors and legislators, mayors, and municipal officials. The federal district is a hybrid of a state and county, similar to how Washington, D.C., is a separate district within the state of Maryland. But Brazil has not always been a republic; it has had many forms of government since its days as a colony.

In the latter part of the nineteenth century, coffee became Brazil's top export and leading money crop. The vibrant economy prompted nearly a million Italian immigrants to come to Brazil looking for work and a better way of life. The country was essentially ruled by rich coffee plantation owners, and in 1889 they supported a military overthrow of the monarchy, forcing Pedro II into exile.

In 1889, the wealthy coffee magnates backed a military coup and the emperor fled, ending Brazil's monarchy. For the following three decades, the coffee growers wielded huge power in the country and had a huge influence on the government. Although a republic, it was basically ruled by the military as a dictatorship. Freedom of the press was curtailed, the army was the ruling authority, and elections were manipulated. Then, when the 1929 stock market crash plunged the world into a depression, the demand for coffee plummeted. The coffee growers lost their fortunes and their power base.

In 1930, Getúlio Vargas staged a coup and took over the presidency. It was supposed to be a temporary position, but once in power, Vargas invoked emergency powers and disbanded the legislature, repealed the Constitution, and replaced the state governors with his own followers. After an unsuccessful Communist uprising in 1935, Vargas took over as a full dictator. His leadership was marked by extreme brutality. Tens of thousands of people were imprisoned, political opponents were sent to isolated holding camps, and government officials commonly used torture. During World War II, Vargas sent German, Italian, and Japanese immigrants to concentration camps.

After the Allied victory in Europe and the U.S. victory in the Pacific Theater, Vargas was overthrown by a military coup that returned the country to a democracy. General Eurico Gaspar Dutra was elected and assumed the presidency in 1946. Looking to rebuild the country after years of dictatorship, Dutra organized a Constituent Assembly to write a new constitution, which was officially made public on September 18, 1946.

Dutra's administration responded to the growing popularity of Communism by outlawing it as a political party. The Brazilian government also passed a law prohibiting the right of acknowledged Communists to hold elective offices. To further emphasize the rejection of Communism, he broke off official relations with the Soviet Union in 1947 while simultaneously strengthening political bonds with the United States.

In an ironic twist, Getúlio Vargas was democratically elected and became president in 1951. But without the complete control he had as dictator, Vargas broke down emotionally under the strain of having to deal with a legislature and political opponents, and in 1954 he committed suicide. Over the next several decades, Brazil went through more political instability with military rule and dictatorships. At last, in 1985, a presidential democracy was reestablished.

Under the Brazilian constitution, revamped in 1988 and 1994, there is an executive branch, a legislature,

FYI FACT:

Brazil is the world leader in electronic online voting, with 100 million voters casting their ballots via the Internet.

Brazil's judicial branch is composed of federal, state, and municipal courts. Pictured above is the Court of Justice in Pernambuco.

and a judiciary. All government workers, except elected officials, have to retire when they reach 70 years old.

To be president, a nominee must be a native Brazilian and at least 35 years old. The president serves a four-year term and can run for a second term.

There are four main political parties—Worker's Party (PT), Brazilian Social Democracy Party (PSDB), Brazilian Democratic Movement Party (PMDB), and the Democrats (DEM). Voting is mandatory for adults 18 to 65 years of age.

The Brazilian Supreme Federal Tribunal, the equivalent to the U.S. Supreme Court, was the first court in the world to transmit its sessions on television and can now also be found on YouTube. In December 2009, the Supreme Court started using Twitter to send out court calendars and decisions.

A capuchin monkey snacks on corn. Brazil has more species of monkeys than any country on earth. In 2007, researchers discovered a new subspecies of monkey in the Amazon rain forest. They named it Mura's saddleback tamarin after the Mura Indian tribe.

The Land

Brazil's expansive land area is divided into four climatic regions: the southern states, the coast, the Brazilian plateau, and the Amazon Basin.

The southern states include Paraná, Rio Grande do Sul, and Santa Catarina. This region lies outside the tropics and has a temperate climate. Occasionally, cold fronts blowing up from the Antarctic can cause temperatures to fall low enough for frost, but snow is very rare.

The Amazon Basin is the largest equatorial area in the world. Annual rainfall in most areas of the basin is over 6.5 feet (2 meters). The "rainy season" lasts all year long near the mouth of the Amazon—there is no dry season. The rainiest months are from December to May. In the southern portion of the basin, the rainiest months are May to August.

The Amazon rain forest, also called Amazonia, produces around 20 percent of the earth's oxygen. It accounts for over half of the planet's remaining rain forest. Amazonia also contains 20 percent of the world's freshwater. The Amazon River ranges from 1 to 35 miles (1.6 to 56 kilometers) wide and dumps 28 billion gallons of water into the Atlantic every minute (1.8 million cubic meters per second).

In 2007, a team of Brazilian scientists claimed to have found the source of the Amazon River—a mountain in southern Peru—making the Amazon 4,225 miles (6,800 kilometers) long instead of the listed 4,080 miles (6,566 kilometers). The added length would make it the

Of the five freshwater species of dolphins in the world, the pink Amazon River dolphin is considered to be the most intelligent. Brazilians call pink dolphins *botos*. These dolphins are an endangered species.

longest river in the world. Despite the findings, the Nile is still listed as the longest river at 4,160 miles (6,695 kilometers) in length. What is not disputed is that the Amazon is the largest river in terms of area covered and amount of water it holds.

The temperature in the Amazon Basin is also consistently warm, averaging between 80 and 90°F (27 and 32°C). Higher temperatures are rare, but the combination of high heat and relentlessly high humidity make it extremely physically uncomfortable. It never gets cold enough to frost in the basin, although in some areas in the southernmost portions it can get as cool as 50°F (10°C).

The Brazilian plateau lies below and to the east of the Amazon Basin. The plateau's average height is between 2,000 and 3,000 feet (610 and 915 meters). The highest portion of the plateau is near the Atlantic coast and slopes lower to the north and to the west as it nears the Amazon River and Paraguay River basins.

Most of the plateau's rainfall—on average 60 inches (150 centimeters)—occurs during October and April. The northeast portion of the plateau gets half that amount of rain and can even suffer occasional droughts. In general, the coast is rainier during the winter; the inland has more precipitation during the summer months.

The east coast of the plateau, which includes Rio de Janeiro, typically has a hot tropical climate, although there are significant differences in the season of greatest rainfall from north to south. The Atlantic coastlands of Brazil are narrow, nestled against the high eastern edge of the plateau. The only lowlands on the Atlantic coast are located around the mouth of the Amazon.

Amazonia, the inland Pantanal wetlands, and the marine life in the coastal areas combine to make Brazil the world's most biologically diverse country. It is home to a third of earth's biodiversity, with 1,300 species of fish, over 1,000 species of birds, 400 mammal species, and 30,000 varieties of plants. Where the Amazon meets the Atlantic Ocean lives a rich variety of wildlife such as giant river otters, freshwater river dolphins, turtles, manatees, and piranhas.

The rain forest is divided into layers, and each has a distinct ecosystem that is home to a unique group of plants and animals. The main layer of the rain forest is the canopy—the "roof" formed by the tree branches—that may be home to half the world's species, including an estimated 30 million types of insects. The canopy is habitat to harpy eagles, monkeys, reptiles, and leaf-cutter ants. It is so thick that only about 20 percent of sunlight gets through its layer. The forest floor, the lowest layer, is a murky world. Only 2 percent of sunlight filters down to the floor, which is covered with decomposing vegetation and organisms that provide food for insects and grubs.

By 2010, one fifth of the Amazon rain forest had been destroyed, and destruction was continuing. Logging, mining, and agriculture are mostly responsible. Without ecological programs, some scientists predict the earth's rain forests could all be gone before 2060.

FYI FACT:

The arapaima, or pirarucu, one of the largest freshwater fish in the world, breathes air through a lunglike organ. This Amazon river fish averages eight feet (2.4 meters) in length and weighs more than 300 pounds (130 kilograms).

Many farmers in Brazil see their produce in local farmers' markets. Among the typical produce grown are eggplant, bananas, pineapples, guava, mangos, papayas, and oranges.

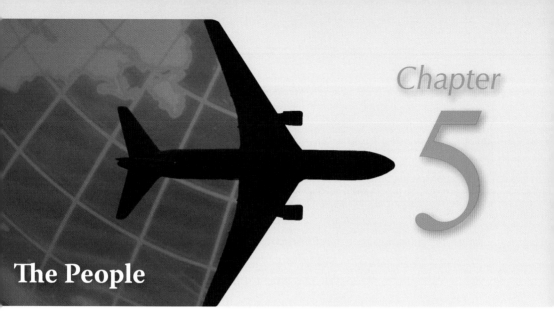

The People

With an estimated 186 million residents, Brazil is the most populous country in Latin America. A third of the population is under sixteen years old. Eight out of ten Brazilians live in urban areas, concentrated in the southeast region of the country. The São Paulo metropolitan area has 19.6 million people; Rio de Janeiro's metro area is home to over 10 million citizens. By comparison, the country's capital, Brasilia, is a relatively small city of 2.5 million.

The majority of Brazilians live near the coastal regions. The expansive interior remains sparsely populated. The country's indigenous tribes live mostly near the Amazon Basin close to the jungle. It is estimated that only 200,000 Amerindians remain.

More than almost any other country in the Americas, Portuguese settlers intermarried with the indigenous population as well as with African slaves. Africans also married native Indians. The result has been a heritage that is truly a melting pot of ethnicity and races. The majority of modern Brazilians have European, African, Amerindian, Asian, and Middle Eastern genetic ties.

Portuguese remains the official language, with a distinct Brazilian dialect, influenced over the years by local African and native Indian dialects. English and French are common second languages. The indigenous populations still speak their native languages.

The Europeans also influenced religion in Brazil. Among the early settlers were Roman Catholic missionaries who worked to convert both the Amerinds and the enslaved African population. The influx of

Italian immigrants further increased the Catholic population of the colony. Brazil has no official religion, but with an estimated 122 million Catholics in the country, the Catholic Church continues to wield significant political and social clout.

Despite the efforts of the missionaries, the African people continued to practice their native religions, which evolved into new forms of worship, often influenced by Catholicism. These beliefs and practices are known generically as Macumba sects. Among the most common of the sects are Umbanda and Candomblé. Followers of Candomblé were persecuted for centuries, but their religion is now recognized as a legitimate form of worship.

Candomblé, which is also practiced in other parts of Latin America, worships deities called Orixás. (They are somewhat analogous to Catholic saints.) A high priest or priestess presides over Candomblé rituals, which include trances, dancing, singing, and, at the end, a meal shared by all the participants.

Education is just as important to Brazilians as spirituality. The country's education system is broken into three levels: fundamental, intermediate, and higher. Fundamental education is compulsory for children 7 to 14 years old. Public schooling is free. There is also pre-school available for children under 7 years old. The school year lasts approximately six months. The fundamental education level covers eight grades. Intermediate education is also free at public schools but it is not compulsory. Higher education, which stresses science and the arts at universities, is also part of the public school system. Founded in 1920, the Federal University of Rio de Janeiro is the largest federal university in Brazil and includes a College of Medicine, Old Academy of Medicine and Surgery, Polytechnical School, and Law School.

Schools in rural areas may have several grades in the same classroom, and classes may be scheduled around the planting and harvesting seasons, so children are free to help their families tend the fields.

Brazilians are raised with a strong work ethic, and with an appreciation for enjoying down time. They celebrate some of the same holidays as those in the United States, including New Year's Day and Christmas. Because of Brazil's location near the equator, the Brazilian New Year happens during their summer. Traditionally, Brazilians dress in white to bring good luck. After ringing in the New Year at midnight, many of them take a traditional dip into the ocean, jumping seven waves and throwing flowers into the sea while making a wish. This is also done to bring good luck and fortune.

Many Brazilian holidays are religious in nature, such as Ash Wednesday, which is the beginning of Lent; All Souls' Day; and a holiday honoring the Virgin Mary.

The national holiday, called Tiradentes, is a weeklong celebration that honors Joaquim José da Silva Xavier—known as Tiradentes—Brazil's first revolutionary against Portuguese colonial rule. Inspired by the American Revolution, Tiradentes urged Brazilians to pursue independence and led a protest in 1789. He was arrested and executed on April 21, 1792. Today, Tiradentes is considered a national hero.

Tiradentes, Portuguese for "tooth-puller," was so named because Xavier was a dentist by trade.

Alferes JOAQUIM JOSÉ DA SILVA XAVIER
'O TIRADENTES'

Brazilian weddings are lavish affairs, filled with unique traditions. For example, the bride must be ten minutes late, dinner tables at the reception have the names of Brazilian cities written on them, and Caipirinha, the famous Brazilian cocktail, is always served.

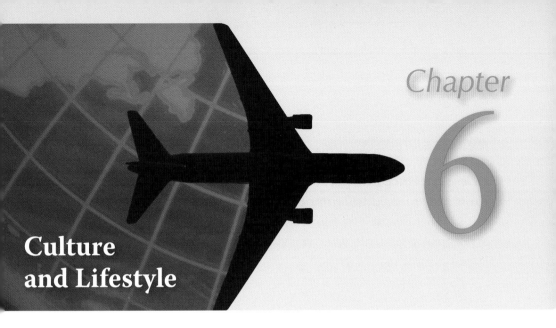

Culture
and Lifestyle

As in many Latin American countries, women have had to struggle for equal rights in Brazil. Culturally, men are viewed as authority figures both in the workplace and at home, and women are seen as subordinate. Traditionally it is a male-dominated society with a double standard when it comes to relationships. If a man has an affair, his wife is expected to accept it. If a woman has an affair, she risks being kicked out of the house and, in some cases, killed. Many men have killed their wives in so-called crimes of passion and not been prosecuted.

In addition to social inequality, Brazilian women have struggled to achieve legal equality. Women did not get the right to vote until 1932. Until the 1960s, women were not considered independent adults. They needed permission from their fathers or, if married, their husbands to leave the country. They were not allowed to own property, and there are fewer women in local and national politics than in any other Latin American country. Although several laws have been passed to protect women from spousal abuse, the lack of enforcement remains a problem.

When it comes to race, Brazil is a nation of contradictions. Even though slavery was legal at one time, discrimination was never legalized. Interracial marriages were common and culturally accepted. But there was still social inequality, with non-whites earning half as much in wages as whites. Even though race was not a political issue, there was clearly prejudice in the workplace that prevented non-whites from advancing professionally.

Historically, black Brazilians who descended from former slaves have experienced the least advancement. In 1931, the Brazilian Negro Front was formed to promote equal rights for blacks but did not generate much interest—or many members. In 1936 it reinvented itself as a political party but was forced to disband after the government outlawed all political parties.

In the late 1970s a new group formed called the Movement for Black Unification, but it wasn't until 1995 that the government officially acknowledged the problem and for the first time established a task force to develop ways to help Brazil's non-white citizens. Even so, the income disparity continues. Brazil, one of the top ten economies in the world, has the most disproportionate distribution of wealth and income of any country.

What Brazilians do not share in wealth, they can share in the country's culture. Music is an integral part of life in Brazil and is very much informed by its African heritage. Dances such as the samba and

Salvador de Bahia musicians and dancers let loose.

Guararapes
International Airport
in Recife, Brazil

Brazil has over 4,200 airports, the second highest number of airports in the world. The United States has the most with more than 14,000.

bossa nova originated in Brazil, along with lesser known dances like batuque, forró, and maxixe—the latter is often called the Brazilian tango. Dance clubs are very popular, and local pubs often feature live music.

Even more popular than music is soccer. Brazilians are zealous sports fans but are positively passionate about soccer and have some of the top players in the world. The national team has won the World Cup five times—more than any other country. Children learn how to play soccer almost as soon as they learn how to walk. In the same way that baseball is said to be America's pastime, soccer is Brazil's athletic obsession.

The arts are also important, especially a tradition called *literature de cordel,* which means "literature on a string." It refers to the custom of hanging pamphlets of rhymed verse by string. The custom remains

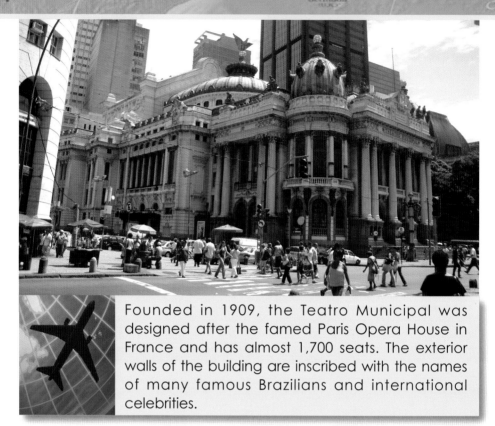

Founded in 1909, the Teatro Municipal was designed after the famed Paris Opera House in France and has almost 1,700 seats. The exterior walls of the building are inscribed with the names of many famous Brazilians and international celebrities.

particularly popular in the northeast region. Cordel performers put together the booklets then recite or sing the verses, which can be used to pass along current events. Afterward, they offer the pamphlets for sale.

As a people, Brazilians are physically affectionate, and it is common to greet one another with hugs or friendly kisses on the cheek. Their culture is less formal with authority figures. For example, instead of calling a physician Dr. Smith or a teacher Ms. Jones, Brazilians would say Dr. Tom and Ms. Jennifer—as long as they were in the same social class. If they are of different social standings, such as an employee to an employer, the body language is subservient and the conversation formal.

Families are close-knit and follow the more-the-merrier philosophy. Family get-togethers include not just immediate family but also extended family, such as cousins and in-laws from both sides. Children typically live at home until they get married, and they will usually settle relatively close to their parents. Surnames reflect this familial closeness. Brazilians typically have two surnames: their father's family name and mother's family name, in that order.

Meals are an important aspect of family life. Brazil's national dish is called feijoada (fay-zwah-AH-dah), which is a bean stew. It is usually made with slowly cooked meat and black beans. The most common foods are rice, beans, and a root called manioc, which is made into a flour that is sprinkled over the rice and beans to make a dish called farinha. Manioc is also used to make *farofa*—manioc flour sautéed with ingredients such as onions, eggs, or olives. Wealthier Brazilians also add beef, chicken, or fish to the dish.

Traditionally, the main meal for Brazilians is lunch. For those who can afford a variety of food, lunch typically includes farinha, an entrée of pasta or meat, and desert. The meal ends with a strong coffee called *cafezinho*. Dinner is a small meal such as a cup of soup or leftovers from lunch. In the major cities, though, the family midday large meal is being replaced. People now commonly eat in restaurants or grab fast food for lunch.

Feijoada can include meats and vegetables.

São Paulo is the seventh largest metropolitan area in the world. People from São Paulo are known as *Paulistanos*. The motto of their city is *Non ducor, duco*—I am not led, I lead.

Economy and Commerce

Brazil has one of the top ten economies in the world and has a growing middle class. Its $1.5 trillion economy exceeds India's and Russia's, and its per-capita income surpasses China's.

Even so, the country still suffers from widespread poverty. Over 30 percent of Brazilians live below the poverty line. And the poorest areas of the country, not surprisingly, suffer the highest crime rates. As Brazil's economy strengthens, the chasm between the poorest citizens and the rest of the country continues to widen.

Compared to the United States, Brazil has a high cost of living. Food and other basics are cheaper, but utility and telephone costs are much higher. Appliances also have a high price tag. Brazilians pay some of the highest tax rates in the world. Women in Brazil carry a heavier financial burden than men because their salaries pay 30 to 40 percent less than men's salaries.

On the other hand, Brazil is investing in its economic future through programs such as Bolsa Familia, a kind of food stamp program. To receive the benefits of the programs, the family's children must stay in school. Low-interest loans are also available for first-time homebuyers and small businesses.

The largest employers in the country are the oil company Petrobras; wholesale fuel brokers BR Distribuidora; the two telecoms Telemar and Telefónica; and brewer AmBev. The top industries are agriculture, mining, and manufacturing.

Arabica is a species of coffee originally grown on the Arabian Peninsula. Scientists believe *Coffea arabica* was the first type of coffee to be cultivated. In Arabia, it grows all year long; in Brazil, the trees can be harvested only in winter.

Brazil is the world's leading producer of sugar and provides approximately 30 percent of all coffee consumed in the world. The discovery of untapped oil reserves was expected to make Brazil one of the globe's biggest producers of crude oil. It is estimated that since the turn of the twenty-first century, around 20 million Brazilians have lifted themselves out of poverty thanks to emerging industries such as production of biofuels.

Ecotourism is also a growing industry. The government hopes that by increasing interest in Brazil's natural resources, it will spur both international tourism and domestic ecology awareness. Since the 1970s, ranching, farming, and gold mining have destroyed an estimated 18 percent of the Amazon rain forest. Education has proved ineffectual so far because Brazilians living in or near the rain forest are poor and are more concerned with the short-term financial needs of their families than the long-term destruction of the forest. It is hoped that the money generated by ecotourism can allow people to earn a living by preserving nature.

Tourists hire local guides and visit remote villages where they buy handicrafts made by local artisans. As a result, many new jobs have been created, and the practical value of saving the rain forest is better understood.

Since 2005, the Brazilian government has announced steady falls in the rate of deforestation and has increased the number of protected reserves, which cover around 35 percent of the Brazilian Amazon. It has also established a national forestry service.

One of the more unique occupations in Brazil is the *castanero,* a worker who collects pods from Brazil nut trees. The trees produce cannonball-sized pods that weigh as much as five pounds (2.3 kilograms) and contain between 15 and 25 Brazil nuts, or *castanas.* Each Brazil nut tree can produce hundreds of pods.

The weight of the pods makes collecting them a dangerous job—falling pods can crush *castaneros.* Unharvested pods are a favorite food of large rodents called agoutis, the only animal able to crack the pods open to snack on the seeds. Brazil produces approximately 39,400 tons (40,000 tonnes) of nuts a year.

FYI FACT:

A Brazil nut is not a nut—it is a seed with a hard concrete-like shell. The Brazil nut contains so much fat that it can burn like a candle.

José Bonifacio de Andrada e Silva was a writer, a scientist, and a statesman. He is credited with discovering four minerals, including petalite, which led to the discovery of the element lithium.

Famous People

Brazil is home to many internationally known statesmen, entertainers, artists, and athletes who have helped shape the country's culture and reflect Brazil's rich traditions and history.

Carmen Miranda

Carmen Miranda was one of Hollywood's first famous Latin actresses. She was born Maria do Carmo Miranda Da Cunha on February 9, 1909, in the small Portuguese town of Várzea da Ovelha. When Carmen was still an infant, her father moved to Brazil and settled in Rio de Janeiro. He opened a barbershop, and the rest of the family joined him.

When Carmen was fourteen, her older sister Olinda contracted tuberculosis. After Olinda was sent back to Portugal for treatment, Carmen quit the convent school she was attending and got a job in a tie shop to help pay the family's medical bills. Her next job was at a boutique, where she learned to make hats. Soon, she started a hat making business.

What she really wanted to do was be a performer. She loved singing and would frequently perform for her coworkers. Her father strongly disapproved of her desire to work in show business. However, her mother supported it. Carmen tried out for a weekly radio show and was hired. In 1928 she landed a recording contract, and over the next decade she recorded over 300 songs.

Carmen Miranda

Her popularity as a singer led to a film career, first in Brazil and then in the United States, where she was known as the Brazilian Bombshell, famous for fruit-filled hats and headdresses. Although she was one of the highest paid movie stars of the 1940s, she was stereotyped as the life-of-the-party Latina. By the end of the 1940s, her career started to decline and she returned to performing in nightclubs.

After years of health ailments, she died on August 5, 1955, at her home in Beverly Hills, California. When she was buried in Rio, nearly one million people turned out to pay their respects.

Joaquim Maria Machado de Assis
Novelist and poet Joaquim Maria Machado de Assis is widely regarded as Brazil's foremost literary figure, although he is virtually unknown outside his country. His best known work is *Memórias Póstumas de Brás Cubas.*

Machado de Assis was born in Rio de Janeiro in 1839 to a mulatto father, who worked as a house painter, and a native Portuguese mother, who died when Machado de Assis was a young child. The grandson of freed slaves, Machado de Assis was a sickly child and suffered from epilepsy. He received little formal education but learned to speak French from a neighbor. He became a printer's apprentice at the National Press when he was

Joaquim Maria Machado de Assis

seventeen and later got a job as a proofreader at Paulo Brito Bookshop. In his mid-thirties he began working at the Ministry of Agriculture and spent many years as a civil servant. He married Carolina de

Novaes in 1869. They had no children, but it was a happy marriage by all accounts.

He began writing in his twenties, and his poetry earned critical acclaim by the time he was twenty-five. But his writing developed a greater depth after he suffered health problems in the 1870s that required a long convalescence. It was during this time that he wrote the novel *Memórias Póstumas de Brás Cubas,* a memoir narrated by a dead man.

In all, Machado wrote nine novels, eight short-story collections, four volumes of poetry, thirteen plays, numerous critical essays, and serialized stories for magazines. In 1897 he founded and became the first president of the Brazilian Academy of Letters.

In his later years, Machado de Assis suffered from failing eyesight and rarely left Rio. He died on September 29, 1908.

Pelé

Edison Arantes do Nascimento was the best soccer player to ever play in Brazil; some say he was the best to play anywhere. He was so good, he needed only one name, and it was known the world over: Pelé.

Pelé was born on October 23, 1940, in Três Corações, Brazil. Of African descent, Pelé's father was a semiprofessional soccer player whose career was cut short by a knee injury. Pelé grew up in Bauru, São Paulo. The family was very poor, and Pelé earned money shining shoes. His father taught him how to play soccer. They were too poor to buy a soccer ball, so Pelé practiced using a grapefruit or a sock stuffed with newspaper.

Even without a proper ball, his talent was evident. By the time he was sixteen he was playing for the professional Santos team and was the leading scorer his first year in the league. He would play for Santos for almost twenty years, winning many state and national championships.

Ten months after turning pro, Pelé was invited to join the Brazilian national team, in the same way professional basketball players are asked to play on the Olympic team. He played in his first World Cup match in 1958, becoming the youngest player ever to compete in the

Pelé played in four World Cups, scoring 12 goals. He is the only player to ever be on three winning Cup teams—1958, 1962, and 1970. Known for his healthy ego, he once said, "I was born for soccer, just as Beethoven was born for music."

international tournament. He also became the youngest player to score a goal and the youngest to score a hat-trick, or three goals in one game. In total, Pelé played with the Brazilian national team in four World Cup tournaments—which, again like the Olympics, are held every four years—with the Brazilians winning three titles.

Pelé retired from soccer in October 1977. The International Olympic Committee named him the Athlete of the Century in 1999. In 1993, Pelé was inducted into the National Soccer Hall of Fame. He published his autobiography in 2007 and devotes time to charity work, especially for children's organizations.

Gisele Bündchen

Brazil has long been known for its beautiful women, so it is no surprise that one of the world's most famous supermodels is from there. Gisele Carolina Nonnenmacher Bündchen was born July 20, 1980, along with her fraternal twin, Patricia. The Bündchens lived in Horizontina, Rio Grande do Sul, a small town in southern Brazil with a population of just 10,000. Gisele says the town had no traffic lights and no movie theater. There was one bank, where her mother worked as a teller, and one hotel.

The Bündchens clearly have the genes for beauty—all five of Gisele's sisters also became models—but growing up, Gisele was considered an ugly duckling. Tall and slender, her classmates teased her and called her Olive Oil, the geeky girlfriend of cartoon character Popeye the Sailor. Gisele laughingly describes herself as looking like a mosquito. She put her height to good use playing volleyball, but sports would un-expectedly give way to fashion.

When she was thirteen, Gisele's mother enrolled her in a modeling class to improve her posture. The class was run by model scout Dilson Stein. In May 1994, Stein took some of his students on a field trip to São Paulo. While there he arranged for executives from the Elite Modeling Agency to meet the girls. One of the executives asked Gisele if she would like to model, but the teen declined the offer. She eventually changed her mind.

"Maybe if my family had been wealthy, I wouldn't have done it," Gisele admitted to *Harper's Bazaar* in April 2009. "But because they weren't—I didn't want to leave

Gisele Bündchen

my whole family, but my parents were working and I had five sisters, so things were challenging. I figured I could be independent and work. I thought I could take care of myself and it would be one less child for them to worry about."

Even though he strongly disapproved of her plan, Gisele's father allowed her to move to São Paulo when she was just fourteen. She shared an apartment with several other models and finished her sophomore year of high school in between auditioning for modeling jobs.

In 1995 Gisele entered the Elite Look Modeling Competition. She didn't win—placing second overall—but it was enough to get her noticed by modeling agent Monica Monteiro, who convinced the teen to leave Elite—considered by some at the time as career suicide—and sign with IMG Model Management. Monteiro became Gisele's mentor and surrogate parent. She drove her to school and at times Gisele lived with her. In return, Gisele did office work for Monteiro.

In December 1996, Gisele spent two weeks in New York City on jobs for Calvin Klein and L'Oreal. Over the following few years she did runway work for many designers—learning English along the way. Her breakthrough year was 1999 when she appeared on the millennium edition of *Vogue* magazine with supermodels such as Naomi Campbell and Claudia Schiffer. *Vogue,* considered the bible of fashion, named Gisele Model of the Year at the Vogue Fashion Awards. She was just nineteen years old.

Modeling led to acting opportunities in the films *Taxi* and *The Devil Wears Prada.* It also led to a high-profile romance with U.S. actor Leonardo DiCaprio and her marriage in February 2009 to professional football player Tom Brady. The couple's first child was born December 8, 2009.

Carnival is celebrated everywhere in Brazil, and Rio de Janeiro, which hosts the world's largest *Carnaval*, is considered the Carnival Capital of the World. An estimated half million international visitors attend Rio's Carnival every year.

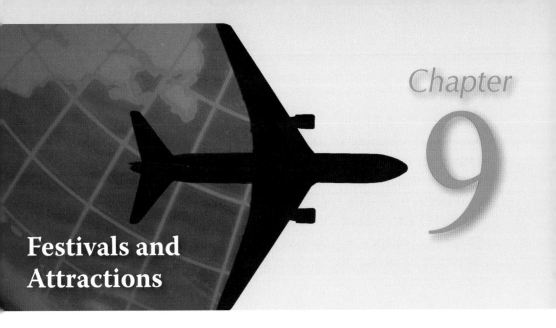

Festivals and Attractions

Whether secular or religious, national or regional, Brazilians take their festivals, and their fun, seriously. Every June Brazilians celebrate Festas Juninas, a midwinter festival that celebrates the feast days of St. John, St. Anthony, and St. Peter. The celebration dates back to the Portuguese settlers and includes games, dances, and traditional foods such as baked sweet potatoes. A pantomime called *Bumba-meu-boi,* or "hit my bull" is performed as part of the celebration. The play is a satire that tells the story of a worker who accidentally kills his boss's bull, which miraculously comes back to life at the end.

In Rio de Janeiro on New Year's Eve, literally millions of people go to the beach to celebrate. The party lasts all day and ends with fireworks at midnight. In addition to celebrating the New Year, it is also the Festa de Iemanjá. Iemanjá is the sea goddess of the native Umbanda religion. She is traditionally given offerings of flowers, perfume, and rice, which are put into small boats on the ocean or just tossed into the water. Giving Iemanjá gifts is supposed to bring good luck for the coming year.

Manaus, Brazil, located in the middle of the Amazon rain forest, is a most unlikely locale for an opera festival, but the Festival Amazonas de Ópera (Amazonas Opera Festival), is one of the most famous opera celebrations in the world. The city's opulent opera house, the Amazon Theatre, is the center of the festival, which takes place every April to May. In addition to the festival, many free concerts are given for Manaus residents.

On the third Thursday of January, the women of Salvador partici-pate in the Washing of the Steps of Bonfim Church. Hundreds of women wearing traditional Bahian clothing wash the church steps with perfumed water. Hundreds of thousands of Salvadorans watch the ceremony.

Brasil Sabor (Taste of Brazil) is a nationwide three-day culinary festival that celebrates Brazilian cuisine. Approximately two thousand dishes are available for sampling from participating restaurants all across the country.

The Festa Nacional do Índio (National Indian Festival) is held every April in the coastal city of Bertioga in southeastern Brazil. The festival occurs in conjunction with Brazilian Indian Day and celebrates Brazil's indigenous people. Tribes participate on a rotating basis in order to give all indigenous groups a chance to take part.

The Church of Nosso Senhor do Bonfim is the most famous church in Salvador. On the second Thursday every January, locals wash the stairs of the church to invite positive energy for the coming year.

A *Mona Lisa*
costume at Carnival

By far the most famous celebration in Brazil is Carnival, a five-day celebration that takes place just before Ash Wednesday, the official start of Lent for Catholics. All five days are national public holidays, and most of the country's stores are closed. Carnival Rio takes place on the last day of Carnival and is the Brazilian equivalent of Mardi Gras in New Orleans, although on a much larger scale.

One of the more spectacular attractions is Beach Park located near the city of Fortaleza. The centerpiece of Beach Park is a water park that features waterfalls, a wave swimming pool, a man-made river, and a 135-foot- (41-meter-) high water slide. As tall as a fourteen-story building, sliders can travel as fast as 65 miles per hour (105 kilometers per hour) on their way down.

Christct the Redeemer over Rio de Janeiro is one of the most famous statues in the world. It was designed by local Brazilian civil engineer Heitor da Silva Costa and created by French sculptor Paul Landowski. At the base of the statue is a chapel.

We Visit Brazil

Rio de Janeiro—Brazil's second largest city behind São Paulo—is known for its nightlife, its well-preserved tropical rain forests, and its white sand beaches, such as Ipanema and Copacabana. Soccer is a national passion in Brazil, and Rio is home to some of the world's largest soccer, or football, stadiums. Rio's most famous landmark is the statue *Christ the Redeemer,* which overlooks the city. Dedicated in 1931, the statue is considered one of the New Seven Wonders of the World.

São Paulo was founded by Jesuits in 1554. Located an hour inland from the coast, the city became a major coffee-producing region. It is considered Brazil's most cosmopolitan city, on par with New York, London, or Paris, and is known for its designer boutiques, world-class restaurants, and vibrant arts scene. The country's wealthiest people live in or around São Paulo.

Ecotourism is becoming a major growth industry in Brazil. In the state of Bahia on the Atlantic coast, Globe Aware offers a one-week Peace Corps-like cultural exchange trip to Porto de Saipu. Visitors are asked to teach villagers basic first aid, teach simple computer skills, tutor locals in rudimentary English, or offer other assistance. In return, locals show visitors traditional cooking, woodcarving, and native dancing.

The Fazenda Rio Negro is a freshwater wetlands preserve along the Negro River, similar to the Florida Everglades. The area is a research center for domestic and international biologists. Visitors can interact with the scientists while exploring the area by canoe to see local wildlife such as the endangered brilliant blue hyacinth macaw and jabiru storks.

The city of Salvador, located in Bahia, lets visitors step back in time. The region reflects its close ties to Africa, especially in the local music, food, and religion. Eighty percent of the residents are of Afro-Brazilian descent. In addition to the imperial architecture and culture, the main draw to Salvador is its pristine beaches.

For those interested in history, the state of Minas Gerais allows another fascinating look into Brazil's past. In the eighteenth century, the area was a thriving gold-mining community, and splendid cities were built. Now they are preserved historical sites. One of them, Ouro Preto, was built during the time of the Portuguese Empire.

The eighteenth-century Church of Our Lady of Pilar is located in Ouro Preto. The city got its name after Portuguese miners discovered black pebbles in a nearby river. The pebbles turned out to be mineral-encrusted gold nuggets, so they named the town Ouro Preto, which means "Black Gold."

 Manaus is a modern city located in the heart of Amazonia. Visitors can take jungle cruises and day trips outside of the city to see how people in river communities live.

Only the most adventurous of tourists go on an Amazon River excursion. Most trips offered last five days and go from Belem to Manaus. The conditions are rustic; travelers sleep in hammocks and there are no creature comforts. It is hot and insects are numerous. But the river trips offer a view of the Amazon rain forest in its purest form.

Whether you visit Brazil for its colorful cities or the ecology of the Amazon, this Latin American country has plenty to explore. You can experience the fun of Carnival in Rio de Janeiro with delicious food and dancing or take an adventure through the streets of historic Ouro Preto. You may even choose to take a ride along the longest river in the world with the help of a native guide. Whatever you decide, you'll find yourself wanting to behold all that this beautiful country has to offer.

Quindim

Quindim is a very popular Brazilian coconut pudding dessert. Here is a typical recipe, although there are many variations depending on the region of Brazil you are in.

Ingredients
8 ounces granulated sugar
3 ounces flaked coconut
1 tablespoon butter, softened
5 egg yolks
1 egg white, beaten until stiff

Directions
1 Preheat the oven to 350°F.
2 Lightly grease a 9-inch pie dish.
3 Mix the sugar, coconut, and butter in a large mixing bowl.
4 Add the egg yolks one at a time while beating with an electric beater.
5 Add the egg white and mix well.
6 Pour the mixture into the pie dish and place in a large roasting pan filled with about 1 inch (2.5 centimeters) of boiling water. Bake for 30 minutes or until golden brown.
7 Allow to cool, then refrigerate until well chilled.

Bottle-cap Tambourines

Make and shake these tambourines, which are popular in Brazil and Africa.

Materials
Strong, Y-shaped branch, preferably hardwood
Dozen metal bottle caps
Hammer
Nail
Strong wire
Acrylic paint and brushes
Assorted decorations: feathers, colored cord, or
    beads

Directions

1 Decorate the stick with
   paints and feathers.

2 Flatten the caps with a
   hammer, then use a nail to
   punch a small hole in the center of
   each cap.

3 Thread the caps onto the wire.

4 Wind the ends of the wire around the arms of the Y,
   keeping the wire taut.

1500   Pedro Álvares Cabral discovers Brazil on April 22. He calls it Island of the True Cross.

1532   First colonies are founded at São Vicente and Piratininga.

1554   Jesuits found São Paulo.

1727   Coffee arrives in South America.

1763   The capital is moved from Salvador da Bahia to Rio de Janeiro.

1822   Pedro I declares independence from Portugal on September 7.

1888   Slavery is abolished in Brazil.

1889   Monarchy is overthrown.

1893   Brazilian civil war starts in the settlement of Canudos, state of Bahia. It will last until 1897.

1930   After a brief revolution against the military, Getúlio Dorneles Vargas is given almost unlimited control over Brazil.

1932   A Brazilian civil war erupts when the state of São Paulo tries to secede. Women gain the right to vote.

1954   After he is asked to resign, Vargas commits suicide.

1960   Capital is moved from Rio de Janeiro to the newly created inland city of Brasilia.

1961   Parliamentary system is established.

1977   Divorce is legalized.

1992   Rio hosts Earth Summit, where nations gathered to discuss improving the health of the planet.

1997   Constitution is amended to allow the president to run for reelection.

2000   Brazil celebrates its 500th anniversary.

2002   Brazil wins the World Cup for fifth time.

2004   Brazil sends its first rocket into space.

2009   Dam failure causes massive blackouts in Rio de Janeiro and São Paulo.

2010   Brazil reaches the quarterfinals of the World Cup but loses to the Netherlands.

Books

Berkenkamp, Lauri. *Discover the Amazon: The World's Largest Rainforest.* White River Junction, VT: Nomad Press, 2008.

Deckker, Zila. *National Geographic Countries of the World: Brazil.* Washington, D.C.: National Geographic Children's Books, 2008.

Riner, Dax. *Pelé.* Brookfield, CT: Twenty-First Century Books, 2010.

Shields, Charles J. *Brazil.* Broomall, PA: Mason Crest, 2009.

Works Consulted

Angus, Michael. "Citizen Emperor: Pedro II and the Making of Brazil (1825–91)." *History Today,* June 1, 2001.

Bishop, Elizabeth. *Brazil.* New York: Time, 1962.

Cavendish, Richard. "Cabral Discovers Brazil." *History Today,* Vol. 50, Issue 4, April 2000.

Central Intelligence Agency. *The World Factbook:* "Brazil."
https://www.cia.gov/library/publications/the-world-factbook/geos/br.html

Conniff, Michael L., and Frank D. McCann. *Modern Brazil: Elites and Masses in Historical Perspective.* Lincoln: University of Nebraska Press, 1991.

Forero, Juan. "Booming Economy, Government Programs Help Brazil Expand Its Middle Class." *Washington Post Foreign Service,* January 3, 2010. http://www.washingtonpost.com/wp-dyn/content/article/2010/01/02/AR2010010200619.html

Fry, Peter. "Politics, Nationality and the Meanings of Race in Brazil." *Daedalus,* Volume 129, Issue 2, 2000.

Goldberg, Isaac. *Brazilian Literature.* New York: Alfred A. Knopf, 1922.

Levine, Robert M. *The History of Brazil.* Westport, CT: Greenwood Press, 1999.

Macaulay, Neill. *Dom Pedro: The Struggle for Liberty in Brazil and Portugal, 1798–1834.* Durham, NC: Duke University Press, 1986.

Mirabella, Marina. "Brazil Hopes New Push for Ecotourism Can Help Save Amazon Rain Forest." *CNN,* January 28, 1998. http://www.cnn.com/TRAVEL/NEWS/9801/28/amazon.ecotourism

Roach, John. "Amazon Longer Than Nile River, Scientists Say," *National Geographic,* June 2007. http://news.nationalgeographic.com/news/2007/06/070619-amazon-river.html

Vincent, Jon S. *Culture and Customs of Brazil.* Westport, CT: Greenwood Press, 2003.

Wilson, Anamaria. "Gisele: Supermodel Muse." *Harper's Bazaar,* April 2009.

On the Internet

Brazil: Country Facts, Information, Photos, Videos
http://kids.nationalgeographic.com/kids/places/find/brazil/

Brazil Football National Team
http://www.footbo.com/Teams/Brazil

Kids Corner Brazil
http://www.kidscornerbrazil.org/

Time For Kids: Brazil
http://www.timeforkids.com/TFK/specials/goplaces/0,12405,104221,00.html

abdicate (AB-dih-kayt)—To formally give up power.

Amerinds (AM-ur-inds)—Short for *Amerindians,* the native peoples of the Americas.

consecration (kon-seh-KRAY-shun)—A religious ceremony held to induct someone, such as a king, into office.

convalescence (kon-vuh-LEH-sents)—Period of healing and recovery.

coup (KOO)—The forceful overthrow of one's government, usually by the military.

ecotourism (eh-koh-TOR-ism)—The business of catering to visitors who come to study the ecology and wildlife of an area.

indigenous (in-DIH-juh-nus)—Native to or naturally occurring in a particular area.

morphology (more FAH luh gee)—The form and structure of a creature.

mulatto (moo-LAH-toh)—Someone with parents of different races.

regency (REE-jen-see)—A person or group chosen to govern in place of a monarch or other ruler who is absent, disabled, or still too young to rule.

seminomadic (seh-mee-noh-MAD-ik)—Of a lifestyle that involves moving temporary dwellings, but having a base camp at which some crops are grown.

spousal (SPOW-zul)—Having to do with a husband or wife.

subservient (sub-SER-vee-unt)—Showing extreme obedience.

surrogate (SUR-uh-get)—A substitute; in place of another.

terrain (tuh-RAYN)—The shape and texture of the land in a particular geographic area.

Kathleen Tracy has been a journalist for over twenty years. Her writing has been featured in magazines including *The Toronto Star*'s "Star Week," *A&E Biography, KidScreen,* and *TV Times.* She is also the author of numerous books for Mitchell Lane Publishers, including *The Story of September 11, 2001* and *We Visit Cuba.* Tracy lives in the Los Angeles area with her two dogs and African Grey parrot.